THE NIGHT FOLDS

BILLIE ARTHUR

COVER: OIL PAINTING BY RYAN BUECHNER

ACKNOWLEDGEMENTS

It is with humility and a deep sense of undeserving (two virtues that were engrained in me by my well-intentioned mother, the word of her god clutched firmly to her chest) that I write this. I carry with me the distinct smell of woodsmoke twisting in the dying pines. I sit between two small hours, perhaps having overserved myself Cabernet Sauvignon. I carry with me that pungent taste, along with immense gratitude. I am compelled, therefore, to pay my devoirs.

I thank my angel in New York who has never allowed distance or time to dampen his support for this conception. Craig, your passion and wisdom inspire me. Your resilience emboldens me. I toil to match your unyielding devotion and strength. I adore you, in this life and in each one to follow.

I thank my darling in Portland for the cover of this book and much more. Ryan, you amaze me. I know no one more kind, no one more tender, no one more earnest. These, Love, are what make your life a treasure. It is my privilege to share in it. Thank you for being my friend.

I thank the illustrious Pacific Northwest for spreading its arms wide for me on the bourn between one life and another. I could not have chosen a better venue to host my awakening. I have never called any one place my home, and I expect I never will. Still, you are unreservedly an intimate companion to me, my long-awaited playmate.

I thank, with pause, the ship who riotously passed me in the night. Though I carry still the bitter taste of you, Daisy, in the back of my throat, I could not be so negligent as to deny your impact, as to ignore the dregs of you. It was beside you that I acknowledged my gift, beside you that I cast light on my dark corners, beside you that I set fire to horrors to which I vowed never to return. Stranger, I wish you no lasting harm.

I thank, with restrained pride, the author. Billie, you steal each day like an unblushing thief. What a contrast to the person you were some years ago, foolishly censoring her existence, as well as her work. You are here — unshrinking, unfinished. Well done.

When will the sun kiss my shoulders?
Or will my fear of flaying
Restrict and remand me to my cellar
Where all pining quietly perishes
With not a fight or feeble cry?

Yearn ever I for the tender licks
Of languid saltwater on my skin,
Longing only still for warm sand
Stuck to my sinews.
So pleasant a dream and widely separate
From the black treacle round
My ankles acting as shackles.

THE
NIGHT FOLDS

THE NIGHTCRAWLER

He sits on my chest. His stature is slight. His feet are massive and icy. His eyes are black. His shoulders are covered in coarse hair. His paws are cumbersome. They cover his knees. His breathing is deep. His throat rumbles with husk. His teeth are jagged, protruding past his taut, cracked lips. They drip with thick, slimy spit. The splashes seep through my sleep shirt.

I try to move, dislodge him, but this only seems to anger him. He huffs and inches his filthy foot out over my ribs. He leans forward; we are nearly nose-to-nose. The weight of his small, wretched form comes down on my sternum. The bones resist. They cry out in pain. The cracks and crunches echo in the moonlit room.

I shut my eyes and pretend that this is just sleep paralysis. But he and I both know that he is as unimaginary as the crust in the corners of my eyes and the sweat pooling under my arms. He is real — from the hair on his back to the stench in between his toes.

He does leave though, only slowly. He dismounts clumsily, hobbles away heavily. He sidles up on the windowsill, but before he is gone, he turns to me. The pale light of the moon illuminates the hollows of his eye sockets. He promises to return. As to when, however, he does not reveal. He is sliding down the side of the house now. He grunts when the grass below catches him. I swallow audibly.

MY GARDEN

I am embittered and sick
With rage at the prospect of
My persistence on this planet.

I do not yet possess the will to eliminate myself.
Each day I move closer
To harnessing the disregard
For how this fateful, unchangeable action
Will flower behind me.

In the midst of my waiting
The resentment is palpable.

I seethe in all my useless puttering about.

THE FLAME

I have a sick obsession with watching
Fortunes fall apart under fire.
Flames dance recklessly.
Ashes fall wantonly.

The darlings I hold dear cannot withstand
The wavering, erraticism of existence.
Yet I keep these brittle bundles
Trapped in my burning forests.

I am a parasitic being with the audacity
To take more than I ever deserved.
In order to destructively consist.
In order to unapologetically persist.

Is this my singular purpose and action?
Am I the only one on fire,
Licking the edges of beauty that
I have no right to taste?

You are an inheritance, Dear Land,
Whose soil is sublime, exquisite.
I wear this knowledge daily.
It is the sludge on the soles of my feet,
The filth beneath my fingernails,
The enmity behind my ears.

I strive to cherish your amulets.
I want to nurture your treasures.
Keep them safe.
Leave them unharmed.

I have been entrusted with the shores,
The hamlets, the fauna —
Those stretching and those crouching.
I would much sooner stab myself a dozen times between
The ribs before squandering your offerings.

When I fade, I should be so lucky
As to lie here, decay here.
Please, then, scatter me
And allow me the courtesy of dissolving
Among these heirlooms.

I have lived selfishly.
I have taken more than to which I had rights.
I have been greedy and green-eyed.
I have existed without decency.
You must have seen.

Restore my dignity
If you could spare the time.
Grant me the sweetest, darkest peace
That which is beside you.

I want to drink deeply of your waters
But I am afraid
I will choke.

I want to fall into you
But I am afraid
I will drown.

I want to gorge myself on you
But I am afraid
I will drink myself ill.

I want to take in your sweetness.
Hold it close to my chest
But I am afraid
I cannot keep you.

If I drink from your well
I am afraid
I will selfishly use you up and
Leave you dry and barren.

I am afraid
I will poison you.

I am afraid
I will get so intoxicated by your waters that
You will become disgusted
By the way I stagger,
Grow annoyed with the way
I stammer and slur.

I am afraid
I will take you in too quickly,
Greedily, gulping, spilling,
Leaving my top a sopping mess.
And you will have gone by then.

I am afraid
I will not be able to recall your richness
On the back of my tongue.

I am afraid
They will cut me off from you.
Rip the bottle from my sticky, sweaty palms.

I am afraid
Of the inevitability of your departure,
That I will forever be
Painstakingly withdrawing from you.

I am a vessel never full.
Tiny holes there are in my feet.
Pinpricks no one can see.
Thin cracks there are along the seams.
Etched from falling so frequently.

I am a vessel never full.
I only sit on a sill.
Catch the light of the sun.
Pray it flatters me so.

I shy away from a touch,
Terrified I will break and spill
All over the carpet,
That the children will puncture their tiny feet
With my sharp-edged organs.

I want so desperately, so naïvely,
To be carried off by the wind,
To be taken away to the sea.
Laid to rest there
Gently, finally.

I would not, however, sink
For my lungs would be relieved.
My bones unburdened.
The weight of persistence would wane.
The trouble of existence would at last be no more.
The heaviness of air would crush me no longer.

I watch with eyes like crystals
As clouds collect above me
Like healers' hands, like the hands of a mother
During the small hours.
I have been wailing for years.
My lungs were burning,
Screaming behind my ribs,
Slowly turning to dust from the agony.

"Please, Mama," I have pleaded.
"Take me in your arms and pat me down.
Dry me off until the residual rattling of my life is lulled,
Until the land has lost my scent."

You must find pleasure in my suffering.
You have your hands round my neck.
Your fingers are tight.
Your thumbs are insistent
As they press against my windpipe.

You like to squeeze until my vision dances
And constellations bloom on the ceiling.
You release, for you wouldn't dare
Let me any nearer to what
I want more than anything.
You would never allow my fingertips to taste.

You like me here:
Suspended between animation and cancellation.
My pain is succulent.

How could I ever love a personage so vile?

Perhaps this is not personal.
Perhaps you strangle all the idealistic girls.
Perhaps they too walk around with bruised throats,
Unable to swallow without discomfort,
Hiding their agony behind turtlenecks,
The petrified tremble of their hands

Inside trouser pockets.

Black spots on my brain,
Blinding me of the things
I would quite like to say.

My tongue is cottoned.
My fingers drip
With the mess of my thoughts.

I lie them out to dry in the Sun,
Liberate them from the wet weight
Clinging on in shadow.
If the Sun could just lick them over,
Might heat their bellies,
I could lift them again, maybe untangle them.

Though perhaps the words, once bone dry,
Will be unintelligible.
I would have wasted so much time in this pursuit.
Time I can never get back.

SINK UP / DRIFT OFF

The sky is piquant, moreish.
She is baby smooth
And softer than a sigh.
I sweep my fingers
Over her milky, plump cheeks.
They bleed.

I would like to swim
In her, so I bend my knees
And I ascend.
She spreads her arms, eager to embrace.
She welcomes me, envelops me
In her warm waters.
I am spilled.

I roll round in her bedsheets,
Placid and unhurried in waking.
On my back with eyes closed,
All is sedate.
Buttery.
Lush.
Time trickles.

I pry my eyes open and there is nothing
To behold but the palatial blue, not even
A suggestion of solid matter.

I will continue floating,
Drifting away until I
(My memory, my stain)
Am but a hint,
A breath,
A murmur.

Loneliness is
Distinctly wet,
Distinctly sharp,
Distinctly wrong,
Distinctly cold.

Solitude, though, is a gift.
My divine privilege and
The reason for my secret smile.
Solitude is distinctly mine.

I can float on solitude, dip my toes into it.
I can drift with it.
I like to sink into solitude, feel it
Surround me on all sides.
I pry my lips apart once I am submerged.
I take it in, fill myself with
Solitude's endlessness.

Quickly, though, it becomes clear
That I have overindulged.
I want desperately to take in
The sweetness of land air but somehow
I am on my knees at the seafloor.
I am tangled in wet strands.

Loneliness is
The sharp realisation that I could die down here.
It is the ache in my lungs —
Their screaming.

I am among those lucky enough not to need
But I occasionally find myself
Painfully in want and keening,
Though for what I am not certain.

I am invisible and it is my honour
To thrive in the dark.

Incorruption there is in the silence.
In the shadows I am solid.
I am real.

But without warning, the stretch is too vast.
The silence is much too loud.
The darkness grips too tightly.
The emptiness bites.

How can something so hollow be so heavy?

I so stupidly craved warmth in my chest and
On my skin like the kiss of sunlight.
I wanted to dance on the edges of canyons.
Hurl axes through the air.
I so vainly wanted to prove that life was a delicacy.
Yet still, my palette is unrefined.

My skin is charred.
My spine is fractured.
My limbs are useless and
Twisted in unnatural ways.
The axes have bounced back,
Blades separating my flesh cleanly.
My blood surges.
The pressure is oppressive.

Apathy, then, is perhaps
The sweet silence of snowfall,
The delicate shade under
A tree in summer,
The soft dark under bedcovers,
The shared secrets between lovers.
It is petrichor.

I pray, though to a prism,
That this apathy is not deadly.
I pray, though to a hologram,
That the snow does not bury me,
The sun does not shift,
The duvet does not smother me,
The secrets are not poisonous.
I pray, though to a spectre,
That the rain does not burn.

DISCIPLINE

I have been silencing myself and retreating
As I find myself absolutely allergic
To my own endless lamenting.

Stale is the smell. It loiters.
Spoiling all, I move
To fetter myself as I find
That I am declining
Whilst you are ascending —
No doubt, the natural course of things.
So brilliant you are.

I must consider that perhaps
You have allowed me to latch
For as long as I have
Because you know not your worth.

You are the sun.
I cannot in good conscience cloud over you.
I will not go on souring your taste of this wide, rich world.

You have had enough darkness,
Enough bitterness,
Enough hate to fill a riverbed.

In short, what remain are these avenues:
Stifle myself,
To which I am obliged.
Drown myself,
To which I am compelled.
Bury myself,
To keep my filth from touching you.

I am engulfed in dismay.
It surrounds me suddenly.
Settles densely.
Locks soundly.
No man can breathe
With the ocean on his back.
My ribs scream when I try.
They threaten to shatter as I infect the inky deep.

At first the plunge seemed like a thrill.
The pull and attraction of the rippling veneer
So darling in the way it sparkled.
It had a winsome glow from where I stood
Like a pervert, mouth watering with anticipation.
I was so high, so deluded, so arrogant
When I leaped.

It was easy to laugh in the face of danger
When I thought I was untouchable.
It was easy to dive head first into the mouth of the sea
When I thought I was unsinkable.

The laughter dies
When defeat reveals its imminence,
When my soul shrivels up and turns black,
When my lungs disintegrate in tandem,
When the cold void burns.
The laughter dies.

THE INSATIABLE BEAST

This pain is excruciating.
More agonising than the betrayal of my father
Rejecting an inconvenient truth.

The ache is pungent and alive.
Rolling in like waves, I am lulled at times.
The beast comes crashing in, then,
And I am completely consumed,
Tossed about and pulled beneath it.
I am rendered powerless
By this fluid, mammoth-sized agony.

When the tide recedes, I soothe myself
As if I am in my small years.
"Monsters are not real.
This panic-inspiring creature
Has swallowed me too many times.
Surely, it has been satiated."

I have always been wrong
In all the ways that matter;
Right in all the ways no one has dared
To notice or understand.

All is water.
Hovering above my head,
Bubbling beneath my feet.
All is water.

Denser I become as I sink in.
Bluer become the veins in my face.
Darker becomes the pigment
In my blackened irises.
All is water.
Water becomes a wall.
Walls gestate and create more walls.

I am swallowed by the roaring dark.
The thickest silence.
The harshest absence.
I split.
My particles scatter and dissolve
Until all is water once again.

The night folds.

BODY BENEATH STRATUS

I want to reconcile the dark
And the light but sometimes
The dark obscures the light so completely
And for such long stretches of time that I forget
The sun ever shone at all on this starved land.
Its face is peaky,
Fragments hollowed out beside the bones.

The dark eclipses everything.
Drains the vestiges.
What remains of the light
— The strength, the fire, the hunger —
Tries to cling onto what is fixed in place.

Rays of sun hang off the perilous edges of my bones.
Grips my heart in its desperate fists.
The last glimpses of light
— The sweet oranges and purples of a sunset —
Ache, yearning not to be sucked away
With the corrosive dark,
Leaving no trace of their existence.

No shadow. No sunburn.
No warmth to the touch.

Paranoia clings to me like sweat.
Apprehension dictates each step.
Insecurity floods the path.
Surrounds me at the waist.
Renders me motionless.

Did these patterns form
As I grew inside my mother?

Are these dysfunctions somehow a direct result
Of my father's failures of courage?
His doubt and his indecision?
His misplaced loyalties and
His penchant for abating my impact?
His determination to disown the parts of me
He does not recognise?

The psychosis follows me like a stench.
Stews beneath my arms and in the creases of my neck.
Ferments at the base of my spine.
I have been painfully aware of it,
Ashamed of the scent since
Before my chest bulged awkwardly under t-shirts.
Before my limbs ached and stretched.

A chasm has formed.
Inside it flow my fables.
I see beasts in my peripheral and wonder,
Are they there?
I study shadows and am alert to each movement.
I listen closely for mutters
In the cavernous silence.

Each time I submit to these compulsions, the fissure expands.
Who is to say I have not built this swamp in my head
And created my own creatures to fill it?

As the canyon widens and deepens,

I lose sight of my convictions.
Darkness slithers in
And sticks to the walls,
Separating me from my reflection.
It swallows all sound.
The ring of my voice peters out,
Discarding echoes as it grows.
Then comes an absence.
Soon I am unable to recall my timbre.
I have forgotten my face.
Did I ever have one?

This is not melancholia,
Though its clouds often sail in,
Thickening and sinking lower to kiss the earth's cheek.

This is discomfort.
This is skin that binds too tight.
Everything is wrong and inherently offensive.
All is misfitting.

I am sick with worry
That nothing flatters,
That everything clings.
I am dizzy with the clench,
Cringing with each chafe.

I scratch at the surface.
I snag at the fabric with a ragged fingernail
To begin the process of flaying myself —
A necessary moulting
Or else I die in agony,
Asphyxiated by an all-encompassing taut grip.

I tease back the oppressive tags of flesh.
I turn them like stale pages in a book.
I hook under sticky warmth
And coerce away the layers
Until they separate from the muscle.

They lie discarded.
They steep in their bloody filth.
They fester —
Putrid and unwanted.

I always return to you.
I always fall into you
Like a drunk lurching this way and that.
Never steady on his feet or with his tongue.
Always staggering.

You are waiting in the wings,
Meditating in the shadows,
Planning your deadly pounce.

One day I will prevail in disarming you.
One day your scent — the warning of your approach —
Will not make me recoil.
I will not shudder,
For you will not set the temperature.
You will no longer send it into a sharp decline.

You will no longer poison the air as you enter a room
And trigger nausea for all its inhabitants.
The sun will not burn as hot, will not blister pink flesh.

I will have studied your design by then,
Been deemed master of your works and your ways.
I will be immune to your infection,
Unsusceptible to your spell.

One day you will be like a priest without faith.
An attorney without conviction.
A surgeon without precision.
A father without fists.

Solemnly I await the inevitable loneliness
That will grow like wild grasses.
It will crush me.
The damage will be irreparable.

I am weary and disinterested in fighting
Off the merciless, relentless ravaging
That is coming for me.
My bones will not raise me up.
My blood has gone cold.
Everything in this forest has been scorched.
I am decaying.

When the loneliness rolls back in,
Sheathing the sky entirely,
It will not cripple me,
For I am already so frail and weedy.
It will only take a single gust of wind.
A mere caress of the solitude I know all too well.

I will be lifted off my filthy feet
And taken away with nothing left
To prove I existed.
Perhaps I did not.

MARCH

To sit within dark
Beside shining wind
As she caresses a cheekbone.
To sit beside crooning frogs
And serenading crickets,
Beneath the sky as she putters about,
Emptying her change purse.

Amid all this swaying and praying,
There rumbles a stillness in woe.
A silence in agony.
An eerie splitting of seams.

Chaos doles itself over citrusy afternoons
When the sun kisses wintered collarbones.
Over syrupy nights with not a frolic seen,
With not a revelry heard.
Only sometimes soft dark.
Only other times warmth.
Only most times blues and greys,
Bleeding into swallowing black.

Still, the house is on fire.
The drapes disintegrate.
The flames lick the wallpaper and devour the ceiling
Like the brutish parties once did.
Still, we rest in gasoline-soaked hammocks,
Deaf to the wreckage.

I fear the intangible darkness that slips through my fingers
Like seawater in the night.
I reach out for what I believe stretches onward
Yet each time I bend towards it, I lurch
Into the void.

I feel her knuckles tasting my skin —
The edge of my cheekbone,
The downy hair at the back of my neck.
I rise for her, sway into her,
Clumsy but curious to know what she smells like
Behind her ears and between her breasts.

I rock and I stagger like a boat on the back
Of the black ocean —
Hips surging and reclining
Dangerously, alluringly.

I keel. The Dark departs, still and again.
She sprinkles her blouses
And the tendrils of her hair with
A fragrance for which I long.
Ever errant, she is a temptress.

Within the folds of her shadowed cache
I know not what awaits.
My stuttering curiosity
Nooses and heaves me
Toward the edge of the earth's face.

Too many hours were wasted whilst I hurled stones.
How long my naive ear would peer
Just above her lips, desperate to know
Just how cavernous she really is.

I grew ravenous,
Impatient, and enraged.
I was slow to accept that she perhaps had no end,

That her essence would me forever evade.

The Black Nothing
is an inflating tomorrow
In which I care not to swim,
For I see not what poses in her catacombs.

I was always going to leave this way —
Quietly and conspiringly.
Wearing your disappointment round my ribs.
Tasting your dismay in my back teeth.

Whether I had been flying through the wide open sky
Or burrowed in a box beneath your feet.
Either scattered along the open road
Or suffocating amid some distant blue — dark and deep.

Either with fluttering heart in throat
With eyes wide and hands trembling
Or with frozen lungs and silent mind.

It did not quite matter just how I would vanish,
For your grief was inevitable.
For the removal would always bite.

DISTANCE FROM THE SUN

The separation and subsequent solitude
Were always necessary
For me to confirm what I was about
All and truly.

How could I ever trust in my own might
If you alone, and not me, have held these bones upright?
How could I ever believe that I enjoyed life
If I was gulping you down between each bite?

Tentatively I have tasted what I believe
Is the essence of life.
It is hard to swallow.
The shape of it clogs my throat.
I choke.
The flavour is bitter, impossibly so.
I hasten to forget,
To wash myself clean of it.

Gratitude is in order.
That which I could never dismiss.

Happiness is not a luxury.
Happiness is a god damn human right.

Yet I find you there and also here
Falling backward into poison-lined traps
With which you are all too familiar,
Losing sleep and with biting teeth,
Bated breaths and cautious steps.
I mourn for the shades of your reflection
You are reluctant to accept.

Here you are now,
Unfettered and twenty years lighter,
Tasting tomorrow on the cusp of your tongue.
Grazing her — ever so ginger —
With the edges of your bitten fingertips,
Craving more of what is supremely sweet
Yet absurdly bitter.

The desire so violent your fists fly.
Your teeth clench. Your nose flares.
Your throat splits when you plead.
Though you have held not her weight.
Though you have heard not her song.
Though you have not yet bathed in her light.
Even still, she is yours to savour.

She is yours.

The sky is low,
Stout and depressed.
She cannot be bothered
To tidy her things.
She chainsmokes and tucks us in with her
Noxious vapours
The smell lingers.
The earth glistens.

Those who have never felt an English gale
Will grizzle over of her spirit.
They will beg her to get dressed,
Pack her things, and go.
They will wonder where went
That girl with hoop earrings,
Her cavernous dimples and winsome smile.
They will ask why she no longer
Wears her whimsical skirts.

What happened to her bouncy ponytail
And her silly barrettes?
They miss her collarbones and the soft
Suggestion of cleavage.
They want to see her knees
And the silk-covered canvases of her calves.
They want to see her dancing again.
They want to see her red toenails.

But I do not mind if she floods the streets with
All the garments that do not flatter her.
I will not tell her to calm down when
She lays into building bricks
With her tearful fists.
I will not be annoyed when she pulls my hair
Or shoves me around.

I will not pout
When she completely shrouds me

In the secrets of her mind.
Drenches me in the sopping anguish
She keeps anchored to the sea floor.

I will only raise my hands
And dance beneath her weeping.
I will bottle up her sorrows.

And on the days when she sparkles
And tugs on the eyes of everyone,
When all the boys chase her,
I will sit back silently and watch that too.

Your spine has been stretching this way
Since the teeth were falling out of your head.
There once was a time when you
Insisted on shrinking yourself,
Trying to fit into fabric that
Was never designed for you.

What a privilege it is, then,
To catch the maxims you permit
From your grisly Yesterday.
To see you bite your tongue
Before ever allowing another
Loth apology taint the air.

To behold your defiance.

How succulent!
Your brazen mouth and blatant stride,
Parading about under the sun.
No longer petrified to plume in the light.

How stunning!
The sway of your wild hair and wide hips.
Your cadence as you curse
Anyone who made you believe that you mis-fit.

Truant are the times when you
Calmed your thought dances,
Hushed the colours of your soul,
Dulled the shape of your mind.

To witness your existence
Plead no pardon —
How lustrous!

Billie lives in Washington, USA. She was born on Friday, the sixth of January 1995. This is her first book.

AMERICAN SPIRIT

I shrank and teetered on the edge
Of a fag, closed my eyes, and took a step
Beyond it until I was all at once
Whisked away with a wispy thread
Of white smoke from my slender cigarette.

I swam in the Great Black Emptiness
For all of Autumn's haunted stretch.
Savouring not a sip of Summer sweat

Nor the tepid taste of penitence.

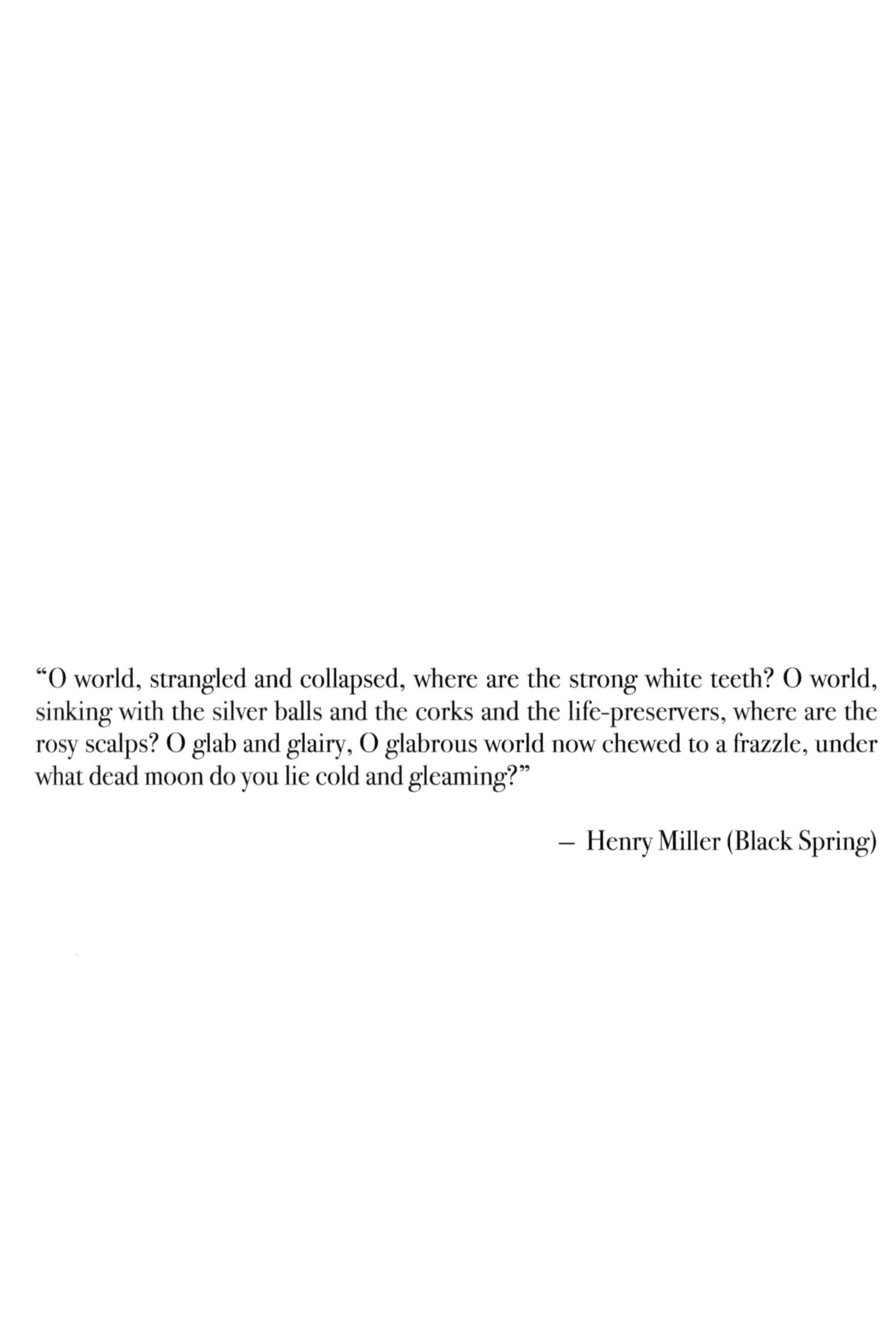

"O world, strangled and collapsed, where are the strong white teeth? O world, sinking with the silver balls and the corks and the life-preservers, where are the rosy scalps? O glab and glairy, O glabrous world now chewed to a frazzle, under what dead moon do you lie cold and gleaming?"

— Henry Miller (Black Spring)

9 798663 815055